# Foreword, by Richard Evans, Director

Without a doubt the tramway at Beamish is one of the
estimate travel in numbers approaching 1.5 million pas
a vital part of our Museum's function as it disperses and
It is this diverse role that makes the tramway so appeali
of historic tramcars, some of which are over 100 years o...,  ....
demanding tramway route linking key areas of the site together. It is no exaggeration to say that
Beamish could not have grown to the size it is and on the scale it aspires to without the tramway.
So it is with great pride that we can look back on forty years of development, from those first
bold steps that set Gateshead 10 on its first trips from Foulbridge to the Town, and also look
forward with the Museum at a point of embarkation on a development plan that seeks to make
it one of the greatest open-air museums in the World. And needless to say, these plans include
the tramway as a central element of the site transport system.

The dedication of staff and volunteers, like those of the Beamish Tramway Group, is key to the
success of the tramway, and also its longevity – it cannot go unremarked that this 1.5 mile route
has been in operation much longer than many tramways built at the turn of the last century. We
are very proud of our tramway and we know our visitors are too. One only has to ride aboard
one of the open topped trams on a hot summer's day and listen to the delighted conversations
around to appreciate this. Likewise the grateful murmur from a tramstop queue on a cold
Christmas evening as the welcoming glow of a tramcar approaches to carry them onwards on
their journey.

I hope that you enjoy this book, which sets out the history, and background to, the Beamish
Museum Tramway, and remember that you too can become involved in its operation and
development – just ask any of our friendly tramcar crews how to get in touch!

# Acknowledgments

Inevitably in the production of a book like this there is a host of people to thank, their
contributions being invaluable in the creation of a written record. But the book itself is an
acknowledgment of the efforts of dedicated staff and volunteers, those with a vision and those
who carried out civil engineering and exceptional restoration to create a World-class heritage
tramway. It is to all of these that this small volume is dedicated.

Nick Meskell is well known for his filming work of Blackpool trams and production of TRAMS
magazine and the tram DVDs which appear quarterly. It is he and his team that has turned
pages of raw text into the book you are holding now and we're sure that you will agree that he
has done a fine job. Also available in 2013 is a DVD to accompany this book and which was
filmed over several events in 2012/13 and includes the fortieth anniversary celebrations.

In the production of this book the following individuals are gratefully thanked: Les Brunton,
Peter Barlow, Tony Wickens, Melvyn Whatmough, Andy Martin, Nick Meskell, Jason Cross,
Dave Hewitt and Paul Jarman.

# Introduction
## *'It won't be a long-term commitment, just about six weeks of advice'*

These were the words proffered to Les Brunton by Beamish Museum's founder Frank Atkinson in 1972. Forty years later Les, and indeed the tramway, are still here having met the ambitious challenge of creating an electric tramway, from scratch, in six months. Thus the Beamish Tramway concept was created and in 1973, it became reality as Gateshead 10 embarked upon its first test trip from Foulbridge to a site earmarked for the then future Town development. 10's journey took place to the sound of a stuttering diesel powered generator, feeding the overhead line and enabling 10 to collect enough power to make this historic first journey. It was the beginning of something that was to grow, like Beamish Museum itself, into one of the foremost attractions in the north east and at the time of that first tentative trip, who on board could have imagined that forty years later this tram, on a much expanded tramway, would play such a key role in one of the World's leading open-air museums.

For many years trams were an accepted part of the everyday street scene, but - perhaps because of this familiarity - little attention was paid to their role in town life. Yet during a period of rapid urbanisation, the trams were the main form of local transport: in spite of opposition they provided fast, cheap and convenient services which profoundly influenced the expansion and development of our towns.

From the pioneering days of the 1890s to the 1920s, electric tramway systems flourished and expanded, and the number of trams in service in the British Isles grew to over 14,000. Thereafter, in the face of under-investment, increasing road congestion and competition from motor buses, trams suffered a severe decline. Some of the larger tramways modernised in the 1930s, but many succumbed to trolleybus or diesel bus operation. After the war the number of trams in service had fallen to 6,000 with

*Newcastle 114, with Les Brunton (left) and Peter Barlow (right) at Pockerley. This is the first incarnation of Newcastle Corporation livery carried by 114, later modified during its 2011 overhaul and repaint.* **Les Brunton**

most remaining systems in a deplorable condition. Despite further modernisation in some cities, notably Glasgow, Sheffield, Liverpool and Leeds, by 1960 only 440 trams remained in use. By the end of 1962, only Blackpool was still operating its tramway - which it retains to this day. The virtually tramless 1960s and 1970s saw also the complete abandonment of trolleybus operation in this country; however there followed a resurgence of interest in light rail systems and their environmental advantages. From 1980 there has been a steady rise in the number of operating systems. Tyne and Wear Metro, Docklands Light Railway, Manchester Metrolink, South Yorkshire Supertram, Midland Metro, Croydon Tramlink and Nottingham Express Transit are all now operating . Edinburgh Tram is under construction, future systems are at various planning stages, and Manchester Metrolink, Midland Metro and Nottingham Express transit are all currently extending their routes, while Blackpool has modernised its infrastructure and introduced a new tram fleet.

The Beamish Tramway, opened in 1973, serves to re-create the experience and atmosphere of tramway operation of an earlier generation, whilst providing an essential means of transport for visitors around the site. The Tramway now handles around 1.5 million passenger-journeys annually, placing it as the busiest heritage tramway in the UK.

Forty years is a significant period of time, and as Richard Evans alluded to in his foreword, it is longer than many tramways operated for commercially. That these four decades have been achieved is all the more remarkable when the age of the tramcars used is taken into account. It is also an anniversary that seems appropriate to celebrate with both a historic celebratory event on the tramway itself, and also with the production of this record of the tramway's history, its genesis, development and story of its fleet of historic tramcars.

The production of a book and celebration of a significant anniversary is by no means a suggestion that the tramway is complete and that there will not be a further forty years (and more!) development to record. But that will be for an author in the future to write! In the meantime we hope that you enjoy this history, find the story inspiring and the technical information sufficient to satisfy your curiosity. If you want to join us in shaping

*The town crossover during replacement with longer radius turnouts. The view shows clearly the construction method for the tramway track in the town as well as the inevitable upheaval such work creates!* **Les Brunton**

the tramway's next forty plus years, you can volunteer and train for operational duties or assist with the restoration and maintenance work. For more information contact the Volunteer Officer via the Museum website or telephone 0191 370 4000. If you are curious about what we will do next and want to keep up with the latest news from the Beamish Tramway (and other transport collections) then you will find a wealth of information on the Transport Blog at www.beamishtransportonline.co.uk

# Chapter 1:
# The formative days of Beamish Tramway

Frank Atkinson, founder of our cherished Beamish Museum, is an inspirational and persuasive character. Way back in 1958, Frank (then at Bowes Museum) had recommended the establishment of an open-air museum for County Durham. The concept became regional in 1966 and in May of that year a Working Party was set up. Meanwhile, quite independently, George Hearse – North Eastern tramway author – had approached the Northumberland and Durham Travel Association (predecessor of the Northumbria Tourist Board) suggesting the setting up of a tourist tramway. Bill Butler of that organisation put George in contact with Frank and his Working Party, and the idea of a Tramway at the proposed museum was born. George was also chairman of the Northern Tramway Sponsors, which had already acquired two trams – Gateshead 10 and Sheffield 342 – from the national collection and brought them to the North East for restoration at Consett. They also had in store a quantity of tramway equipment at Brancepeth. 'Beamish' came into existence in 1970, the idea of a tramway soon germinated and Frank established the 'Beamish Tramway Construction Committee' (BTCC) in 1972 to advise on its construction, working alongside the Northern Tramway Sponsors who were to operate the system initially.

At that time, Les Brunton was working as a young recently-qualified Transmission Engineer in Durham District of CEGB (now National Grid Co.). Having an interest in electric traction, trams and trolleybuses, he wrote to Frank offering help and received an enthusiastic reply on 12 April 1972 from Ian Walden (then Keeper of Industry). This explained that Beamish had secured an English Tourist Board grant towards establishing a ½-mile Tramway and Depot by Summer 1973, but had run into programming problems with the power supply. This was followed up by a phone call from Frank, asking if Les could join the BTCC to help to devise a temporary generator for the tramway. Les recalls him saying 'It won't be a long-term commitment, just about six weeks of advice'. Les did indeed join, but is still there forty years later - and the job is not finished yet! The first meeting of the BTCC was held on 18 Dec 1972, at which its purpose was stated "to advise on the construction, maintenance and development of the museum tramway". Les was unable to attend that meeting, but recalls vividly the second meeting – around that enormous polished oval table at Beamish Hall, with gin-and-tonic refreshment. That day, skill areas were identified as Overhead (Peter Price), Electricity Supplies (Les Brunton), Permanent Way (Ian Johnston), Trams (Eric Wailes) and Civils (Dave Rumney).

*Gateshead 10 ventures out on a short section of electrified line at Templetown, Consett. A number of Beamish's transport collections found their way to this safe haven in the late 1960s including the ex North Eastern Railway C Class (LNER J21 Class) No.65033.*
**Beamish Collection**

That is how it all started, but from those tentative beginnings the tramway and its fleet has steadily and continuously developed. The Depot was completed later in 1973 and the permanent substation and Motor-Generator commissioned in 1975, by which time Tony Wickens and Peter Barlow had joined the Group. By November that year it was reported that 96,000 visitors had been carried on the Tramway, and a clear policy was declared to extend it to serve the whole site. Sheffield 342

(264) joined the service at Easter 1976, running initially as an open-topper, numbered '1'. Over the subsequent years further trams have been acquired and restored: Sheffield 513, Blackpool 31, Oporto 196, Newcastle 114 and Sunderland 16, as well as various others on loan. One of the Group's own projects was the restoration of Newcastle Sunbeam trolleybus 501, which was completed in 2004 and is set to come into its own with the projected 1950s area developments. In 1980 the BTCC formally became the 'Beamish Tramway Group'. Members of the Group give their services voluntarily and work directly with the Museum as well as having close ties with the Friends of Beamish. The Group comprises a number of electric traction experts, devotees and enthusiasts drawn from a variety of backgrounds, invited to assist the development of the tramway in several fields. These range from the preparation of technical schemes, operating rules and procedures, to hands-on workshop activity and crewing the trams.

The tramway has been extended three times: into the Town itself in 1975, from Foulbridge to the Visitor Entrance in 1988, then completing the circle to the Town via Pockerley Bottom in 1993. The completed route is now one and three-quarter miles in length, with four passing loops. The permanent tram fleet stands at eight vehicles, from which a maximum of four operate the route at peak seasonal periods. So, from those humble beginnings in 1973, Beamish Tramway now serves to re-create the experience and atmosphere of tramway operation of an earlier generation, whilst providing an essential means of transport for visitors around the site. Today, the Tramway handles over a million passenger-journeys annually, placing it as by far the busiest heritage tramway in the UK.

*Sheffield 264, then in its guise as 342 (for a while 'Beamish 1') was also overhauled at Templetown, where it was converted to open top guise at the request of Frank Atkinson. It also took on a variant of Gateshead livery complete with appropriate adverts.*
**Beamish Collection**

# Chapter 2:
# Phase 1: Foulbridge to the Town

The route for the initial stretch of Tramway was designed towards the end of 1972, at which time Beamish Museum comprised administration offices and an exhibition within Beamish Hall (at the time owned by Durham County Council), a temporary wooden Admissions Building, the 'Beamish begins here' exhibition, the Rally Field and a vast undeveloped site. A Tram Depot was to be built at Foulbridge, connecting via a sharp curve to the initial route which would skirt the Rally Field to a temporary terminus but be quickly extended into the nascent and developing

Town area. Contractors had been appointed at the turn of the year and work proceeded through the winter, despite very poor wet ground conditions. Track laying using recovered second-hand rail from the Depot site down to Town West entrance (there was no 'Town' yet) was completed by 18 March 1973, but the Depot, Substation and public utility power supplies were very much behind schedule. Consequently, when Gateshead Tram 10 was delivered from Consett on 26

*Very early days on site at Beamish. This view today is much changed, the steam navvy offering a datum for comparison with the modern view. The tram depot now stands to the left, with the tramway running away from the photographer on the right hand side.* **Beamish Collection**

April it had to be off-loaded using the body jacks at the temporary top end of the track (just above what is now Foulbridge Crossing). Meanwhile the BTCC had obtained second-hand traction poles and trolley wire from the Bradford Trolleybus system (which had just closed) and had erected overhead wiring from Foulbridge Crossing down to a temporary terminus by the Rally Field. They had also concocted a temporary 550Vdc diesel generator from a former road drill compressor trailer (Gardner engine) driving an ex-Bradford trolleybus motor wired as a generator. This stood by the track at Foulbridge, wired up to the overhead line (positive) through a circuit breaker, and the track (negative).

Tram 10 ran for the first time at Beamish on 17 May 1973, with weekend demonstration runs for visitors starting soon afterwards. The fare was 20p (return!) for which the Conductor issued a ticket from a Bell Punch rack. Driving the tram using the Diesel Generator required an interesting technique. Applying controller power initially 'flattened' the generator voltage, from which it failed to accelerate. So we soon learned that the way to 'surprise' it was to apply power then immediately throw off the controller again, causing the Gardner Diesel to accelerate under its governor action. As it roared back to speed (signalled by impressive smoke-rings seen over the embankment), the driver would re-apply power and the tram would take off!

From this pioneering start, Phase 1 of the Tramway quickly developed. The Depot was completed later in 1973, although it was quickly found that No. 10 could not cope with the sharp access curve, so the present Depot Yard layout and Fouldbridge Tram Stop were soon adopted. The Substation was equipped with its Motor-Generator set in 1975, enabling the Diesel Generator to be retired, and removing power supply restrictions. The

*A view from the charmingly (!) named 'Bog Bend' looking up towards Fouldbridge and the Museum's service centre, workshops and tram depot. The tramway follows the route of the earth track with the events field to the right.* **Beamish Collection**

overhead line was installed over the remainder of the initial track to a temporary stop at 'Town West', where visitors could already see progress with Rowley Station, the Park and the Annfield Plain Co-op rebuild. Over the following three years the track was extended into the Town street as a double track with crossover, to reach the temporary fence just beyond the site of the present Sweet Shop. This extension brought the length of the tram route to just under ½ mile (755m). The overhead work in the Town Street incorporated the two ornate double bracket arms with decorative scrollwork, which had miraculously survived for 50 years in the undergrowth at Newcastle Corporation's Paradise Yard, having been removed from streets in the 1920s!

The scene was now set for a decade of stable operation of the tramway. Having established the Tram Stop at Fouldbridge, the success of the tramway confirmed the determination to extend it to the proposed new Visitor Centre. It is important to recall here that the three Phases of tramway development described were not undertaken over three discrete periods of time. It was more of a continuous development programme, with considerable overlap of phases. For example, Phase 2 works started before the Town Street track doubling was completed, and the start of Phase 3 works pre-dated the completion of Fouldbridge loop on the Visitor Entrance extension. These phased changes all brought an interesting sequence of operational tram service patterns for the discerning visitor!

*The view from Bog Bend looking north and showing the route of the tramway sweeping through the scene on its newly created formation to the area that would become the Beamish Town Street.* **Beamish Collection**

*Newly arrived from Consett, Gateshead 10 is yet to run under its own power at Beamish at the time of this photograph. The tram is stood on the crossing which now enables access onto the Museum site from the office complex.* **Les Brunton**

*Another view of 10, particularly interesting as it shows the wheeled generator to the right (in grey) – the early power supply for the tramway, whose habits are alluded to in the text.* **Les Brunton**

*An overview of the Foulbridge area. Note the original curved approach track to the depot and the grounded tramcar body – a temporary shelter and the remains of a Dick Kerr tram, thought to be ex Tynemouth Tramways and long since broken up.* **Peter Barlow**

The original gateway to Beamish Museum was the 'temporary' wooden Admissions Building, leading to the Rally Field and car park. As the site developed, visitor numbers grew rapidly so the establishment of a permanent Entrance and Visitor Centre facility quickly became crucial. The site chosen was adjacent to the Shepherd & Shepherdess pub in Beamish Village, with later direct access from the A693 by-pass road. As long ago as October 1980 plans were being drawn up, but an important aspect of this commercial development was soon realised to be the exploitation of substantial open-cast coal reserves under the site. Coal extraction proceeded for the next three years, enabling earthworks for the Visitor Centre, large terraced Car Park and Tramway extension to be started in October 1984. The inspiration and materials for the Centre came from the former local Greencroft Hall, which was demolished, transported and rebuilt. Indeed the Tramway extension and Tram Stop were originally referred to as 'Greencroft', until the rather more prosaic title of 'Visitor Entrance' was adopted at opening.

The earthworks for the tramway extension involved considerable land-fill just beyond Foulbridge tram stop, incorporating a culvert to take Letch Burn under the alignment followed by a gentle rising left curve with spectacular views over the developing Colliery and Pit Village area, to reach the new Visitor Entrance Tram Stop and loop. The length of the alignment extension was almost ½ mile (517m), bringing the total length of the tram route to over ¾ mile (1272m). The new

*The first loop at the Entrance (later relaid using Garden Festival turnouts) with 342 and 10 present. The move of the entrance to this location gave the Museum a significant and impressive gateway and created a busy transport hub. Future plans may see an additional loop or siding laid here to increase capacity as the Museum develops new period areas.* **Peter Barlow**

extension comprised a high-specification metalled road with drainage, footpath and a single reserved track ballasted tramway on the outside of the curved alignment. The traction poles were set to the outside of the curve, allowing the use of bracket arms to support double trolley wires for use by trams and trolleybuses. The overhead was erected before track laying commenced (for easier use of our ex-Stockport road tower wagon) and was complete by November 1985. Track laying then started, using initially second-hand rail (this was later upgraded with new 80A section rail), and was completed in February 1986. A test run was made in July 1986 and following an inspection by HM Railway Inspectorate on 17 October 1986 public service commenced to a temporary stop at the top of the Colliery path on 7 October 1986. Opening of the new Visitor Centre itself took place shortly afterwards. At this time Foulbridge loop had yet to be constructed, so the whole route had to be run as one long single-track section;

completion of the loop in June 1988 allowed a more flexible service to be operated. An additional single trolley wire for tramway use was later erected, both to allow independence of trolleybus testing from tramway operations and to provide additional overhead rating in preparation for the Stage 3 extension.

*This view taken from the tower wagon at Foulbridge shows one of the more dramatic landscape changes that the tramway brought about. Beyond the end of the track is a valley, carrying the Letch Burn, down towards the Colliery Village. The Burn now runs through a concrete pipe whilst the valley is bridged by a substantial embankment largely made up of demolition waste from terraced housing in Gateshead.* **Peter Barlow**

*Sheffield 513 and Gateshead 10 create an almost timeless scene at Foulbridge, which by this time had become the mid point on the tramway route as well as hosting the depot and workshops complex.* **Les Brunton**

GAJ 15 heads west from the Entrance towards Foulbridge. This location is much changed today on account of the substantial tree growth and appearance of vegetation to the right of this view. The former Teesside trolleybus No.5 was never operated in service but made numerous forays during its time at Beamish on test runs using the new overhead line, which remains today as the first section of the planned trolleybus circuit of the site. *Peter Barlow*

A shot of the Entrance loop during reconstruction and replacement of the turnouts with ex Garden Festival components. *Peter Barlow*

Journey's end – Gateshead 10 stands outside the printers at the Town Terminus. Note the wooden fence to the right, demarking the then boundary of the Town before the 1990s European funding fuelled a colossal building programme at Beamish. *Les Brunton*

It may seem curious to link Gateshead Garden Festival tramway to the completion of Beamish's circular tram route, but the stories are very closely linked. The account starts in the summer of 1988, when Glasgow had built and operated a tramway at its Garden Festival. At about the same time, the Gateshead Garden Festival team had appointed Newcastle-based consultants Merz and McLellan (for whom Les Brunton then worked) in connection with the establishment of a tramway for its Garden Festival to be staged in the summer of 1990. A commercial arrangement was agreed between Gateshead Garden Festival and Beamish Museum whereby Beamish would install the tramway infrastructure on the Festival site, maintain it during the Festival's 157-day performance, then dismantle and remove it after closure. In return, Beamish would retain the recovered equipment for re-use on its own tramway. After the Glasgow Garden Festival tramway closed, a successful bid was made by Gateshead to purchase and remove some

*The sylvan setting of Birch Wood, rudely bisected by the earthworks for the road and tramway extension. This view, looking down from the Entrance, shows just how much work was required to create the route, on a 1:16 maximum gradient, to the Pockerley tram stop.* **Les Brunton**

of the infrastructure (track, overhead and power supply) for re-use at Gateshead. Construction on the Gateshead Garden Festival site started in 1989, and Beamish Museum duly constructed the tram track and overhead line. The short route linked the two parts of the site by a single open-track section using second hand rails. At each end there were loops laid in grooved rail and points (mainly second hand from Glasgow Garden Festival, with a small Depot at one end (housing the Substations) and a Running Shed at the other. The overhead comprised recovered bracket arm and span equipment (again mainly from Glasgow) supported on refurbished ex-Newcastle trolleybus poles, recently acquired from City Lighting. As these had been burned off at ground level, they were re-extended by specialist welding bottom tube sections from other sacrificed poles; by this method for every three scrap poles two refurbished poles were produced – at a fraction of the 'new' price. The foundations for the poles were designed such that the poles could be easily lifted at the end of the Festival. The three trams for the Garden Festival were all hired from the National Tramway Museum, comprising Newcastle 102, Blackpool 167 and Sunderland 100 (née MET 331). The Festival was a great success and boost for the local economy, including a record 520,000 visitors to Beamish that year resulting from the two organisations promoting joint tickets for visits to both sites.

*A short while later and the road is now clearly defined and the overhead awaits track and trams beneath it.* **Les Brunton**

Meanwhile, back at Beamish, the 1975 dream of completing the circular route had started to become a reality. The Phase 3 route survey was completed in July 1986, showing that part of the existing railway alignment from Rowley to the Colliery (which had never shown promise operationally) could be taken over for tramway use, and that the considerable difference in levels between the Visitor Entrance and Pockerley Bottom could just be accommodated by establishing a curving alignment down through Birch Wood at a gradient of 1 in 16 – the maximum gradient allowed for trams without track brakes by the 1926 Memorandum on Tramways (authority was sought from HM Railway Inspectorate, and granted). Following on from the Phase 2 extension, the alignment was planned to accommodate a footpath, roadway and reserved track tramway. A swathe was therefore cut through Birch Wood, an earthworks contract let in October 1991 and the track centre line pegged out. In the same way as Phase 2, the poles and overhead lines were erected before the track was laid. The wiring was designed for tramway only initially (but with passive provision for a future trolleybus route), and comprised two contact wires (one per direction) spaced close together. This was both to eliminate the need for frogs (overhead junctions) at the loops and to provide sufficient electrical conductivity in view of the distance from the only Traction Substation at the Depot. The poles on Phase 3 are ex-Garden Festival refurbished Newcastle trolleybus poles as described earlier, while bracket arms are proprietary continental units carrying composite Swiss/British fittings. The contact wires are 80mm² SG copper alloy, bought new and erected over most of the extended route on 7 April 1992 from Visitor Entrance via Pockerley to Town East. Track laying followed, the open route track being in new 80A section rail and the loops and point-work recovered from the Garden Festival, supplemented by some material. Meanwhile work was proceeding apace on the track, roadway and overhead equipment in the Town Street on the 'other side' of the barrier fence, co-ordinated with the building works going on at that end of Town. The length of the Phase 3 extension was over ½ mile, bringing the total route length to almost 1½ miles (2.303km).

The overhead was energised in two stages: Town East to 'the fence' on 15 February 1993 and Visitor Entrance to Town East on 24 May. Then, later that day, gauging test runs were made by trams 31 and 196 all the way round the circle. The final HM Railway Inspectorate inspection took place on 8 June and the full circle was officially opened in the presence of invited guests on 24 June by Kenneth Hudson, Director of the 'European Museum of the Year' Award. Pride of place was taken by Sheffield 264, fully garlanded in flowers, which led a procession of trams round the new circular route. Public service started that afternoon, and visitors were immediately treated to a fascinating trip through the Town East building site – a scene that must have been reminiscent of the 1920s, when urban tramways were spreading out into the developing suburbs! From there, visitors were taken right through to the Visitor Entrance initially, as the Pockerley area was still being developed to depict the 1820s; however, the Pockerley tram stop came into use when Pockerley Old Hall was completed in 1995 and subsequently became very busy after completion of the Steam Waggonway.

*Blackpool 31, not long restored from its engineering tram function, pokes its nose around the Town East curves in a view that reveals the construction of the garage and sweet shop as well as new double track running line which would take the tramway full-circle around the Museum.* **Les Brunton**

*One of the two elaborate centre traction poles, adorned with period lights, located in the Town Street.* **Les Brunton**

Opening day for the full 1.5 mile tramway. A garlanded Sheffield 264 waits to break the tape and lead a short procession including 196 and 31 along the extended street and clockwise towards Pockerley, the Entrance and ultimately, the Street once again. **Les Brunton**

**Right:** The ex Stockport Corporation Thorneycroft tower wagon was an unsung hero of the creation of the Beamish Tramway. After completion of the full circle, and a reluctance for the insurers to inspect it as an access platform, it was sold on. It was subsequently restored and converted into a flatbed lorry by its new owner. **Les Brunton**

**Left:** The easiest way to retrieve traction poles is to cut them off at ground level. This, however, leaves them a little on the short side! Here a batch of poles is prepared for the final phase of the circuit development and shows new bases welded into position to restore the full height of the poles. **Les Brunton**

## The Track

Over the years, the second-hand rail originally laid has been replaced by new material. Most of the track now comprises new flat-bottomed BS 80A section railway rail, spiked to base-plates and timber sleepers, with check rails on heavier curves, as 'reserved' ballasted track. Over the years Beamish has benefitted commercially through adding on to existing orders for 80A section rail, sharing production runs with Docklands Light Railway for the Phase 3 extension, and with Tanzanian Railways for later rail replacements on Phases 1 and 2. In the street-running areas however European Standard Ri60 section grooved tram rail is used, set with tie-rods on a reinforced concrete bed, with infill in tarmac, or granite setts in period areas. Grooved tramway rail is no longer rolled in the UK, so has to be sourced from continental Europe. Although some has had to be purchased new, Beamish has benefitted from acquiring rail second hand from Glasgow and Gateshead Garden Festivals, and from joint orders with Wirral Tramway, Birkenhead. The points at loops and cross-overs are all new (or recent second hand) by Edgar Allen Ltd, with 1 in 6 crossings, and sprung turnout blades where appropriate. Trackwork in and around the Depot is in mainly second-hand material though this will be replaced in time. The year-round heavy use of the tramway poses maintenance and renewal demands, undertaken by the Museum's in-house Permanent Way team. Sharing of technical knowledge and facilities with modern UK tramways is a big advantage here, for example, continuous welding in-situ to build up worn tram rail on curves.

## The Overhead Line and Power Supply

The poles supporting the overhead have all been recovered from former tram and trolleybus systems, in many cases restored to their original length by specialist welding (see Page 21). They are three-section stepped circular hollow section poles conforming to the former BS 8, and comprise a range of three diameters thicknesses to provide the duty required for each location. They are set in concrete to a depth of about 6 feet (2 metres). The trolley wire is grooved copper alloy, 4/0 SWG (80 sq. mm), suspended either from bracket arms or on span-wire construction, at a normal height of 21 feet (6 metres). A second (negative) wire is provided in the Depot

*A close up view of the tower wagon in action.* **Les Brunton**

area and from Foulbridge to the Entrance, for safety earthing purposes and for test-running trolleybuses. The trams are all fitted with trolley poles and carbon-slipper trolley heads, and return their traction current via the running rails. Overhead fittings have been salvaged from the Newcastle, South Shields, Tees-side and Bradford systems, and in the Town area period fittings have been used wherever practicable. Elsewhere the opportunity has been taken to use modern French and Swiss fittings, and to prototype test new UK fittings. The line voltage is 550V dc, and the overhead is divided into electrical sections with trackside section and earthing switches to gain maximum operating flexibility and allow partial shut-down of the route for winter work.

The dc power is derived from the Northern Powergrid 20kV / 400V ac incoming mains. 'Beamish Museum Substation' – one of three 20kV public utility substations supplying the site - is located in the Tram Depot and, as well as the traction supply for the Tramway, provides mains supplies for the Regional Resource Centre and Workshops, Home Farm, Visitor Entrance and the Pit Village. The 550V dc traction supply has been provided since 28 March 1988 by a purpose-built 150kW 12-pulse silicon transformer-rectifier set. It is distributed via circuit breakers and isolators to the Depot, Depot Yard, and to the Main Line which is fed by underground cable to Feeder Pillar 1. The circuit breakers now used for feeding the Depot circuits were acquired by Beamish in May 1981 from the Tyne Pedestrian and Cyclist Tunnels, where they had formerly supplied power to the escalators at 480V dc. A Permit-to-Work safety system is used when working on the Substation or Main Line overhead line equipment, and an energisation warning lamp and key interlock system is used for work on or near the Depot Road overhead equipment.

From 1975 until 1988, the traction current was supplied by a 250kW motor-generator set installed in the Substation. This machine is of Bruce Peebles manufacture, supplied initially to the North of Scotland Hydroelectric Board in September 1939, and later acquired by the NCB for use at Settling Stones Colliery. As a 'direct-on-line machine', it takes a large starting current from the mains supply for a few seconds, so was quite unpopular with the Electricity Board when in daily use! The machine was retired in 1988 on conservation and energy efficiency grounds, but remains available on standby.

## The Tram Depot

The Depot is located within the Foulbridge workshop complex (the Regional Heritage Engineering Centre) and includes accommodation for trams on four roads (1, 2, 3 and 4) and for cars, buses and trolleybuses on roads 4 and 5. Road 3 is equipped with an inspection and service pit. Road 1 is currently being prepared for its new role as Tramway Restoration Workshop. Mechanical and Electrical workshops and Stores provide the facilities for routine maintenance, repairs, overhauls and complete restoration work, not only on the vehicles but also on the track, power supply and overhead line system. Although much of the work on the trams is carried out on site, some specialist work such as traction motor overhauls and wheel re-profiling is undertaken off site by local contractors. The Depot also houses the substation and telephone exchange.

# Signalling and Communications

The service pattern varies from one tram in use during the winter season, through two or three during the early summer, to four on high season days. Exceptionally, the whole tram fleet has turned out on August Bank Holidays and for parades and other special occasions. The track layout allows operation in both directions round the circular route, with short-workings at the start and finish of each day's service. The pattern, and changes to it, are controlled by the Tramway Supervisor, who keeps the drivers informed of the passing instructions at the loops. The single track sections are therefore regulated by service pattern knowledge and 'line of sight' working, with one exception. The steep gradient on a curve through Birch Wood precludes the use of 'line of sight'; here control is ensured by a pair of electrically linked 'block token' instruments, located in green trackside cabinets at Visitor Entrance and Pockerley Bottom loops. A driver must collect a token as authority to proceed; removal of a token locks both instruments, preventing removal of another token until the first is replaced. Electrical impulse clocks, driven from a master clock in the Depot, are located at each passing loop in pole-mounted boxes. These also contain telephones connected into the PABX exchange, also located in the Depot. Each tram in service also carries a radio hand-set for normal and emergency site use.

*A number of operational features of the Beamish Tramway are illustrated here. On the left is the case containing the internal telephone system and clock. On the right is the cabin containing one of two interlocked token machines that ensure that only one tramcar traverses the steeply graded and curved Pockerley Bank through Birch Wood. **Les Brunton***

18

*One of the many features of the tramway is its close proximity to the eastern end of the North Eastern Railway branchline in the Town area. Here visiting steam locomotive W.S.T. (from the Bowes Railway) watches Gateshead 10 pass on an anti-clockwise service.* **Paul Jarman**

*The classic view of a Newcastle A class tram in service. Much study of the livery of 114 has taken place, based on knowledge of early film characteristics and the way in which this would render colours. It was concluded that the waist panel, beneath the window, is actually a light colour – cadmium yellow – though the early films, being blind to such shades, cause a dark shade to appear when printed.*
**Beamish Collection**

*Above:* Though the buses have not been covered by this book, the 1987 Daimler replica is of relevance to our story. Until 2012 it carried Gateshead Tramways livery - as the originals had in 1913 when the tramway sought to extend its routes by using connecting bus services. Soon these grew into the mighty 'Northern' - the 2012 repaint reflecting this change. **Andy Martin**

*Left:* Following purchase by William Southern, a Gateshead driver, Gateshead 52 was moved to an allotment in Low Fell where it remained for a number of years before transfer to the growing museum at Crich in Derbyshire, home of the Tramway Museum Society. In 2012 the TMS agreed to transfer ownership of 52 to Beamish, and so in due course this tram will undergo a comprehensive reconstruction in order to join the working collection not so far from its home town.
**George Hearse**

*Opposite:* Blackpool 31 has made two visits to its former stomping ground, the last being in 2010 in connection with the 125th anniversary celebrations of the electric tramway on the Lancashire coast. Seen here on tour duty and heading for the promenade with the famous Metropole Hotel in the background. **Jason Cross**

*Recent years have seen a growth in movement of tramcars between heritage tramways. Sheffield 513, following a lengthy loan to the tramway in Blackpool, was moved to the East Anglia Transport Museum near Lowestoft on a five year loan. In 2012 it was joined for a brief period by another Beamish nomad – Newcastle trolleybus 501. Here the pair are seen together at Carlton Colville, home of the EATM.* **David Jordan**

*The Georgian landscape of Pockerley Old Hall dominates this view of Sunderland 101 (Blackpool 703) traversing the scenic section of line between Pockerley and the Town, seemingly unnoticed by the horses grazing in the field!* **Dave Hewitt**

Leeds 6 arrived for a short working visit in 2010 and ended up staying for 3 years! It proved to be a versatile and rugged tram and was well liked by crews. It is seen here sprinting up the grade on an anti-clockwise service with Pockerley Old Hall on the hillside in the distance. **Dave Hewitt**

Beamish is always a popular night time venue, not least the Town area and especially when the trams are present. Here 16, 10, 264 and 31 fill the street during an evening function on the 13 October 2005.
**Paul Jarman**

Photographic charters, where enthusiasts hire the tramway out-of-hours, have proved to be immensely popular in the last five years with numerous groups attending. Here a group is seen silhouetted against a backdrop of Blackpool 233 and 304 during a night time charter in 2012.
**Andy Martin**

Another photo charter scene – a recreation of the Grimsby & Immingham Electric Railway by night with Beamish's 1933 Morris Commercial and Gateshead 10 (in its G&I guise as British Railways 26) starring.
**Andy Martin**

Another VAMBAC controlled tramcar to visit Beamish was Blackpool 304, owned by the Lancastrian Transport Trust and operated at the Museum during the autumn of 2012. It is seen here with another LTT tram, Blackpool 233, recreating a 1950s scene from the seaside town. **Jason Cross**

*Blackpool 11 was a hugely popular visiting tramcar to the Museum in 2011. Operating for just four days, the superbly restored VAMBAC controlled tram was loaned by the East Anglian Transport Museum for the spring transport event. It is seen here during a photographic charter in the Town Street.* **Jason Cross**

The first operation of a horse tram at Beamish was carried out in 2009, the honour falling to the newly restored Manchester 53, usually based at Heaton Park. Of the Eades reversible design, it was a great crowd pleaser and returned the following year for a further brief spell of operation. It is seen here with a pair of horses plus assisting trace horse in front.
**Paul Jarman**

Cardiff 131 was the first Welsh tram to operate at Beamish and also the first from the National Tramway Museum collection. It appeared in April 2010 as part of the 'Corporations & Contractors' event that spring. **Paul Jarman**

**Opposite page:** In April 2010 the transport event included three former works cars as well as numerous service vehicles and road construction plant. Blackpool 31, midway through a repaint following overhaul, briefly regained its engineering guise as Blackpool 4, though still carrying passengers. The green soon gave way to the 1920s livery and so this scene is probably now history itself. **Paul Jarman**

Gateshead 10, after many requests from enthusiasts and a public appeal for funds, was repainted into its British Railways appearance (carrying number 26) in September 2012. The tram ran in this livery on the Grimsby & Immingham Electric Railway (owned by BR) and is seen here on the not dissimilar reserved track at Beamish, traversing the curve shown on Pages 6 and 7. *Jason Cross*

*Excellent links have been built up with the other UK heritage tram operators. Heaton Park's Manchester 'Combination Car' 765 ran at Beamish for several weeks in April and May 2011, seen here with 10 and 16 in the background.* **Andy Martin**

***Above:*** *In September 2012 Oporto 196 emerged from a heavy overhaul wearing a variant of the long-lost South Shields livery. With appropriate advertising boards the tram re-entered service looking stunning in the blue and primrose livery latterly used by South Shields for its trams.* **Andy Martin**

***Opposite:*** *To round off this section on visiting trams, here is the Merseyside Tramway Preservation Society's Birkenhead 20, which operated at Beamish in March and April 2012 and further increased the variety of other tramway's trams to work in County Durham.* **Paul Jarman**

***Previous page:*** *Leeds 6, formerly Hull 96, is part of the Heaton Park tramway collection and arrived to take part in the Corporations & Contractors gala in April 2010. It subsequently stayed, returning to Manchester in March 2013. It is seen here recreating its nocturnal existence alongside a Fowler T3 steam roller.* **Jason Cross**

## Trams

Since 1973 Beamish Tramway has developed from a short demonstration line with one tram (Gateshead 10) to the present 2013 operation involving up to four from a fleet of eight trams dealing with a million passenger-journeys annually, placing it as the busiest heritage tramway in the UK. Over the intervening forty years, trams have been acquired and restored or borrowed, whilst others in store await attention as future projects. All the operational vehicles are now described, appearing in the same order as they were put into service at Beamish, followed by borrowed vehicles and vehicles awaiting restoration. Here they are described in construction date order.

*Photograph: Beamish Collection*

## Sunderland 16

Sunderland Corporation Tramways No.16 was built as an open-top tramcar by Dick, Kerr & Co., Preston, in 1900, forming with her five sister trams the batch 13-18. As with many other tramway undertakings, Sunderland fitted its early vehicles with top covers, and most of its fleet was so dealt with by 1916. However, No.16 and the others of the same class had to wait until after the Great War to receive this treatment. Many other modifications followed in the 1920s and 1930s: new trucks, new staircases, alterations to the seating, and the substitution of a bow collector in place of the trolley arm.

When the Sunderland tram system closed in 1954, a number of tram bodies escaped the usual fate of burning in a scrapyard, instead finding a new use as football changing-rooms. After a spell on a football field, the lower saloon of No.16 was moved to Westwood Farm, Low Warden, near Hexham, Northumberland, where it spent the next 30-odd years as a tool-shed and apple store.

*Photograph: Jason Cross*

The body was rescued by Beamish North of England Open-Air Museum in 1989 as a potential restoration project, followed by several years' research work, production of engineering drawings and procurement of both materials and specialist services. Three major contracts were let: for the refurbishment of a second-hand Peckham P35 truck, for the reconstruction of the recovered lower saloon, and for the construction of a new top deck from drawings. These three elements came together at Beamish early in 2001, followed by two years' painstaking work to restore this sole-surviving original Sunderland tram to its 1920s enclosed double-deck condition. 16 was launched into service in July 2003, providing a useful 66-seat vehicle for year-round use on Beamish Tramway, whilst representing the second-largest tramway undertaking in the North East.

*16's lower saloon as recovered.* **Les Brunton**

# Newcastle 114

114 is one of twenty four-wheel open-top short-canopied 'A- Class' tramcars built in 1901 by Hurst Nelson and Co. Ltd., Motherwell, for Newcastle Corporation Tramways. As delivered by the makers it had wooden seats for 53 passengers and was mounted on a 6' 6" wheelbase Brill 21E truck equipped with GE 58 motors and BTH B3 controllers. During their lives these vehicles were extensively rebuilt, one of the early improvements being the provision of a top cover for the upper deck seats. The majority of these trams, including 114, were sold to Sheffield Corporation in 1941 following inspection on the scrap siding in Gosforth Park, to replace war-damaged vehicles. After further upgrading to totally enclosed and vestibuled form – a rebuild that reflected great credit on Sheffield Tramways - they performed useful service until final withdrawal in the early 1950s. 114 ran in this form as Sheffield 317 until 1951.

The body of 317 (114) was discovered on an arable farm near Scunthorpe, and after several moves it arrived at Beamish in 1987. Total rebuilding was carried out using a mixture of contract, museum and volunteer labour, and incorporating as many original parts as was practicable. A suitable truck with GE 270 motors was acquired from Oporto in 1989 which was restored and modified to suit 114's dimensions. Two BTH B18 controllers were also collected, rebuilt and installed, and the tram was totally rewired to modern safety standards. The whole restoration project took nine years to complete, culminating in 114 returning to passenger service in May 1996. Sufficient of the original body parts have been retained and incorporated to preserve the tram's pedigree, and 114 now stands as the unique example of this type of tram to survive. Built as it was to replace horse trams, and restored to 1901 form, 114 certainly appears as the most antique of the Beamish tramcar fleet.

*Photograph: Les Brunton*

*Photograph: Beamish Collection*

*Opposite page: Paul Jarman*

# Blackpool 31

Blackpool 31 was originally built as a four-wheel double deck open-top car in 1901 by the Midland Railway Carriage and Wagon Co. Ltd., for use on the Marton route. In 1918 Blackpool rebuilt the car as a trial prior to embarking on the production of its 'Standard' cars. The body was lengthened and fitted to a new underframe; the three large windows show the extent of the original 1901 body and the small window at each end shows the amount by which it was extended. The rebuilt body was placed on a pair of English Electric 4' wheelbase equal-wheel bogies, to the American McGuire pattern. Each carries a BTH 265C 35hp motor, and the tram is equipped with BTH 510 controllers.

The car ran as an open-top unvestibuled tram until 1928, when a top cover was fitted. However in 1934 it was transferred from the passenger fleet to the Engineering Department and the top cover was once more removed. Renumbered Engineering Car 4, the tram was fitted with an overhead line inspection tower in the centre of the upper deck, with two trolley arms disposed

*Photograph: Beamish Collection*

front and rear, and driver's windscreens were added. In the fleet renumbering of the 1960s the car was renumbered 754. The car survived in regular use in this guise, remarkably, for 50 years. Then in July 1984, it was transferred on long-term loan from Blackpool for restoration and operation at Beamish, in part-payment for the loan of Sheffield 513. The restoration work was undertaken over the succeeding three years in the Beamish workshops, and this very popular high-capacity tram now operates regularly every summer as open-platform, open-top double deck Blackpool tram 31 in its 1920s condition. Tram 31 however returned to its native Blackpool for the 1998 summer season to help celebrate the centenary of the Blackpool - Fleetwood Tramway, and has also taken part in short-term loan to the Heaton Park Tramway in Manchester.

*Photograph: Peter Barlow*

40

*Blackpool 31 is seen here decorated for its role in a professional photo shoot to produce publicity material for the Museum's Christmas Festival season. It was fitted with strings of lights as well as floral decorations for this. Note this was before the 2010 repaint and shows numerous detail livery differences to that now carried.* **Andy Martin**

*In September 2011 the 'Power from the Past' event featured a parade of tramcars along the Town Street. 31, then out of service as it was operating on only one motor, led the parade, complete with 'Circular Tour' headboard (a feature seen in Blackpool in the 1920s). The rear was brought up by visiting Blackpool 11.* **Andy Martin**

*Two close up views showing 31's BCT crest and elaborate scumbled and lined paintwork and a detail of the Circular Tour head board based on 1920s examples.* **Both Andy Martin**

# Sheffield 264

264 is one of 15 double deck balcony cars delivered in 1907 to Sheffield Corporation Tramways by the United Electric Car Company of Preston. The body has wooden seats for 54 passengers, and is mounted on a 4-wheel Peckham P22 truck with two Metrovick 102DR 60hp motors operated by BTH B510 controllers. The braking systems comprise a handbrake acting on all wheels, an electric brake for emergency use and a hand-wheel operated track brake. The tram was rebuilt in 1926 with a totally-enclosed upper deck. Then, owing to the large number of new more modern trams introduced by Sheffield, it was renumbered 342 in the late 1930s and relegated to peak-hour use, although it survived in service until 1956. 342 was acquired by the British Transport Commission and exhibited in Clapham Transport Museum until 1967, when its removal to Consett Iron Company premises was organised by the Northern Tramway Sponsors.

342 arrived at Beamish in December 1973 painted in Gateshead colours and temporarily converted to an open top layout owing to the poor condition of the upper deck structure. The tram operated in this form until 1985, when it was withdrawn for a major rebuild to restore it to its 1920s condition as open balcony car 264. This work, which involved the construction of a substantially new top

*Photograph: Paul Jarman*

deck incorporating many original components, and the application of the ornate period Sheffield livery of Prussian blue and cream with gold lining, was completed in 1987. In this form 264 proved to be a most useful all-weather tram, and worked hard for a further 14 years. However, the decision had to be taken to withdraw 264 from service in 2002, pending major restoration work which will involve the construction of a new underframe and substantial rebuilding of the body structure, much of which dates from the tram's original 1907 construction. The tram is therefore currently in store, complete in 'as withdrawn' condition. A restoration report and cost plan has been drawn up, and work is scheduled to commence in the Beamish Tram Restoration Workshop in 2014.

*Having been given a Gateshead style identity, Sheffield 264 (later 342 in this open top condition) is seen outside the Templetown Engine Sheds belonging to the Consett Iron Company. These sheds housed not only 264 and 10, but also other exhibits being collected for what was to become Beamish, including the famous North Eastern Railway J21 class locomotive No.65033.*
**Beamish Collection**

*264 freshly overhauled and complete with its top deck cover once again.* **Les Brunton**

# Gateshead 10

Gateshead 10 was the first tram to arrive at Beamish, inaugurating the initial tram service in 1973. The tram is one of a batch of single-deck cars built during the period 1920 to 1928 by the Gateshead and District Tramways Co. at its Sunderland Road works, and itself dates from 1925. It is 42' 8" in length and is fitted with longitudinal seating for 48 passengers. Its equipment comprises a pair of Brill 39E reversed maximum traction bogies with Dick Kerr DK31A 35hp motors, operated from English Electric DB1 K3 controllers. Air brakes are fitted, which act on the wheels and the track-brakes. The tram worked on routes in Gateshead and across the Tyne to Newcastle and Gosforth, and has a distinctive arrangement of front exit and rear entrance, denoted by the large triangular notice on the dash panels.

When the Gateshead system was abandoned in 1951, tram 10 plus eighteen similar cars were bought by the Eastern Region of British Railways to work on their electric railway between Grimsby and Immingham. Painted dark green, and carrying the fleet number 26, it ran until the railway closed on 1 July 1961. Fortunately the car was retained by the British Transport Commission as a candidate for preservation. In 1968, in anticipation of Beamish Museum, the Northern Tramway Sponsors arranged for the tram to return to the North East. It was restored to its original guise as Gateshead 10 at the Consett Iron Company works, before being transferred to Beamish in 1973. One of its sister trams - Gateshead 5 - can be seen at the National Tramway Museum at Crich, Derbyshire. 10 received a major rebuild between 1983 and 1985, appearing in late 1920s condition, complete with sumptuous woodwork, ornate brass chandeliers, bird's-eye maple ceiling panels, and etched coloured glass advertisements at the top of the side windows. In 2012 it was temporarily returned to its British Railways green livery as Grimsby and Immingham 26; it will be re-painted as Gateshead 10 later in 2013.

*Opposite page: Gateshead 10 at rest outside the tramway depot.* **Paul Jarman**

# Oporto 196

Tram 196 is a small 4-wheel single decker, built in 1935 at the Boavista Works of Companhia Carris de Ferro do Porto (The Oporto Tramways Company) to an American design dating from 1909. It was one of 77 generally similar cars, although the earlier versions differed in length and/or width. The tram is mounted on a Brill 21E design of truck equipped with a pair of GE(USA) 270A 55hp motors controlled from licensee-built B54E controllers.

*Above: 196 during its later working days in Oporto before being shipped to Beamish.* **Les Brunton**

The braking systems include air-brake, emergency electric brake, and a handbrake operated by distinctive vertical hand-wheels to the right of the driver's position. Oporto withdrew 196 after suffering collision damage, and it was brought to Beamish from Portugal in 1989. A number of similar trams of this type have been acquired for preservation in this country and in America, but 196's destiny initially was to yield spare parts for other tram projects. However, once its sound condition had been realised, to the extent that it was capable of running on arrival, Beamish decided to convert it to a totally-enclosed car primarily for off-season operation, and to obtain an additional tram (176, in worse condition) for spare parts. Damaged areas of 196's body were made good, and the former open-sided platforms closed in, with folding door access on the UK loading side. Seating arranged longitudinally for 28 passengers was installed, and the richly-decorated varnished wood features restored. Externally the panel-work was replaced and the original matchwood dashes restored. The original roof-mounted electrical resistances were replaced by new platform-mounted units, arranged to help to keep the car interior warm in winter. Although some changes have been made to the destination boxes, and the tram appeared in the same livery as Gateshead 10, considerable care has been taken to retain the original styling in the alterations carried out (observant passengers will see some notices still in Portuguese). Unusual retained features are the 14 saloon windows, whose two halves open by sliding up into recesses in the roof. 196 joined the Beamish service fleet in May 1992, and had a proud moment a year later when it was the first tram around the completed circular route via Pockerley. 196 underwent a complete overhaul in 2012, emerging in South Shields blue and primrose livery.

*Opposite Above: 196 seen in pseudo Gateshead livery, by now with fully enclosed platforms.* **Paul Jarman**

*Opposite Below: When it was discovered that 196 was in such good condition, a second Oporto tram, 176, was obtained in order to provide its truck, controllers and other equipment for 114's restoration. The body was subsequently sold off, mounted on a trailer and attends some traction engine rallies in the north of England.* **Peter Barlow**

# Sheffield 513

513 is one of a build of 35 double deck trams constructed between 1950-1952 by Charles Roberts & Co. of Wakefield, to a design by Sheffield Transport, having comfortable upholstered seating for 62 passengers. It is carried on a 4-wheel Maley and Taunton hornless type 588 truck with rubber and leaf spring suspension. The car is powered by two Metrovick 101 DR3 65hp motors. Air brakes are fitted, acting on all wheels, and electric braking is available for emergency use. Representing the ultimate development of the traditional British 4-wheel tramcar, 513 worked for only eight years, as Sheffield abandoned its first tramway system in 1960. On 8 October of that year 513 ran specially decorated in the final procession; so too did sister tram 510, now preserved by the National Tramway Museum at Crich. The wheel has now turned full circle, as Sheffield's second-generation tramway - South Yorkshire Supertram - was completed in 1995.

513 was purchased by Mr John Rothera of York, who stored it by the Middleton Railway in Leeds until September 1962, when it was moved to Cullingworth goods shed near Halifax. There it remained until 1973 when Mr Rothera presented it to the Castle Museum, York. No covered storage could be found at York, so after a period of outside storage it arrived at Beamish in

*Photograph: Peter Barlow*

1976. During those 16 years of storage much damage was done. Many windows were broken and panels dented, the leather upholstery suffered and the mahogany mouldings were stained by rain water. One of the controllers and some air pipework had been cut out and removed, the light fittings badly damaged and the air gauges destroyed. Restoration by Beamish commenced in 1978 and the tram was fitted with a pair of Crompton-West CT/TJ controllers, entering service at Beamish in 1983. On 1 October 1984, 513 left for Blackpool where it operated on loan for 14 months, taking part with nine other preserved trams in the Blackpool Tramway Centenary celebrations in September 1985. After several more years' service at Beamish, and a major mechanical overhaul, 513 returned to Blackpool in February 2011, this time for a longer-term loan. As part of Blackpool's modernisation programme, 513 was transferred to East Anglia Transport Museum at Carlton Colville (near Lowestoft) in 2011 where it has augmented their operating fleet of trams and trolleybuses. The planned construction of a 1950s area at Beamish, to incorporate a tram and trolleybus route, means that 513 will return to Beamish in due course.

*Opposite page: Sheffield 513 basks in the sunshine in Blackpool whilst engaged on a private tour.* **Jason Cross**

# Blackpool 233

When Walter Luff took over as Manager of Blackpool Corporation Transport, his 1930s modernisation plan saw the development of a family of centre entrance cars including the Railcoach, Balloon and Open Boat types. The prototype Boat (225) arrived in January 1934 and was followed by 11 production cars (226-236) in July and August 1934, which differed from prototype 225 in having higher sides. Officially titled 'Luxury Toastracks' they quickly became known as Boats, reflecting their Gondola-like appearance with a central canopied entrance and streamlined profile. Blackpool's thrift extended to the use of second-hand control equipment (BTH B18s) in most cars, although most received new motors. 233 entered service on 7 August 1934. As a 'summer only' car, Works records show a routine service in 1941 with a reported very low mileage of just 41,000, so its career mileage is estimated at about 150,000 only. Its duties included the well known 'Circular Tour' which enjoyed a post-war resurgence in the late 1950s, and Promenade 'specials'. The Boats were initially kept at Marton Depot, but in the 1960s they moved to Bispham depot until this closed after which they then relocated to Rigby Road. The initial Boat livery was cream with green waist, front 'V' and canopy, but in 1960 233 lost the green waist and 'V'. The previous winter had seen the application of windscreens at each end to afford some protection to the driver.

The closure of Blackpool's inland routes caused a substantial fleet reduction; four Boats were scrapped but the surviving eight were re-numbered 600-607, our 233 becoming 605. Another round of repaints then took place with a further minor livery change: the entire upper section being green with the rest cream, 605 being so treated in April 1972. The 1970s saw the withdrawal of two more Boats. However, 605 was stored from May 1987 to May 1990, when sponsorship from the Fylde Tramway Society enabled it to be repainted in its original livery. 1993 saw the original B18 controllers replaced by larger English Electric Z-type units, reducing the seating capacity from 56 to 52. 605 was repainted in 1998 into an untypical wartime predominantly green livery for the rest of its service life in Blackpool. Despite being threatened with withdrawal on occasions from 2004 605 ran until October 2009 when it was bought for preservation by the Lancastrian Transport Trust. After storage in 2010 and 2011, Boat 605 left Blackpool on 29 February 2012 and arrived at Beamish the following day on loan. Commissioning followed shortly afterwards and, repainted and carrying its original number once again, 233 entered service at Beamish on 11 April 2012.

*Opposite page: Blackpool 233 enjoys a rare day out during the wet summer of 2012.* **Paul Jarman**

# Sunderland 101

In 1933 when Walter Luff took over as Manager of Blackpool Corporation Transport, he found that he had a fleet of outdated trams so set about modernising his fleet. Firstly he ordered some samples of new trams, one being a 'luxury dreadnought' numbered 226, an open-topped double decker seating over 90 people, and featuring centre entrances with folding doors. The tram was so well received that a further 12 were ordered (237-249) as well as 14 similar enclosed cars (250-263). These trams became fondly known as 'Balloons' because of their streamlined bloated appearance. The Second World War saw a decline in the use of the open-topped Balloons and a need for more closed-topped cars, so during 1942 the open-topped cars were given closed upper decks to match their sisters. One of this batch, 240, is the subject of this description. After the war, the Balloons became neglected, as Walter Luff saw them as being old-fashioned and too slow to load; he saw the way forward as a frequent service using new Coronation single deckers. However, when Joseph Franklin took over as Manager, he saw the potential of the Balloon cars, which therefore started to receive repaints and extra seating capacity, with bench seats being fitted to each end of the upper deck on most of the trams, bringing their seating capacity to an astounding 94. With hindsight, it is lucky that the Balloons were not withdrawn and scrapped, in view of the problems with the Coronations, which caused them to be prematurely scrapped. There were also some minor changes made to the Balloons around this time to modernise them, with most receiving single destination displays at both ends, new rubber mounted roof windows. In 1968 all trams were renumbered, Balloons 237-263 becoming 700-726. 240 became 703.

Car 703 was painted into wartime livery in 1995 to celebrate 50 years since VE Day and also received a trolley for a short time as it retained (and still does) most of the original Balloon features, including curved roof windows. Winter 2003 saw 703 repainted in 1980s livery and it took part in a cavalcade with four others in 2004 to mark the 70th anniversary of the English Electric trams being built. However in 2009, 703 was withdrawn from service and transferred to the Lancastrian Transport Trust. Inspired by its similarity to English Electric tram 99 purchased by Sunderland, 703 was repainted into Sunderland red and cream livery and transferred to Beamish Museum on 15 September 2010 on a five-year loan as a working exhibit, masquerading as 'Sunderland 101'. After an overhaul, remedial work and the reinstatement of trolley current collection, 101 was launched into service at Beamish on 18 October 2011.

*Photograph: Jason Cross*

# Keighley 12

12 (registered WT 7108) is one of four single deck trolleybuses purchased by Keighley Corporation in 1924 to replace its tramcars. It comprises a 32 seat body built by Brush mounted on a Straker-Clough chassis with BTH electrical equipment and a BTH 247 40 HP motor. Current collection is by means of a pair of trolley arms mounted on an Estler Co-axial trolley base - with the parms mounted one above the other.

Originally built with solid tyres, it was later fitted with pneumatics, although this probably represented the major modification during its short service life. In 1931 Keighley Corporation relinquished control of its municipal transport to West Yorkshire, which very soon abandoned trolleybus operation.

Stripped of electrical equipment, No.12 found its way to Grassington, near Skipton, where it was adapted as a holiday home. The body forward of the windscreen was cut away in order to graft on a kitchen/bathroom section, but the remainder was left more or less intact, apart from the erection of internal bulkheads and some built-in furniture. The chassis was left virtually untouched. In July 1988, Beamish acquired 12 and transhipped it to the Museum. Since then, all the alien internal material has been removed, exposing most of the original structure, which appears to be in reasonably sound condition. When resources are available it is intended to restore it to running condition, although it may not be possible to reproduce some of the original equipment.

*Photograph: Beamish Collection*

*Photograph: Les Brunton*

# Newcastle 501

Newcastle Corporation Transport introduced trolleybus operation in October 1935 as part of its tramway replacement programme, and the fleet had grown to over 100 vehicles during the Second World War. Between 1946 and 1949, in an ambitious modernisation effort, 186 new trolleybuses were ordered, both to replace the original fleet and to expand the system to its maximum extent of 37 route miles. Six batches of trolleybuses were ordered, comprising 100 three-axle and 86 two-axle types. Chassis were by B.U.T. and Sunbeam, electrical equipment from English Electric and Metropolitan-Vickers, and bodywork by Metro-Cammell and Northern Coach Builders.

501 is the only survivor of the batch of 30 Sunbeam S7 three-axle trolleybuses, and was delivered on 27 July 1948. Of particular local interest is the timber-framed bodywork, which was constructed by Northern Coach Builders at its Claremont Road, Newcastle, works. 512 of the same batch was exhibited at the 1948 Commercial Motor Show. Based at Byker Depot, 501 operated for 17 years on Newcastle's heaviest cross-city services. These trolleybuses were nick-named 'Coffins' by the crews, as they were six inches narrower than the more modern-looking eight-feet wide B.U.Ts.

Newcastle replaced its trolleybus services with motor buses in stages over the period 1963 to 1966. As part of this programme, the 'Coffins' were withdrawn on 30 May 1965. All were scrapped except 501, which was retained by Newcastle Museum of Science and Engineering and kept for some time at Byker Depot. After spending some years at various storage sites, 501 arrived at Beamish in 1974. Restoration work commenced by the Beamish Tramway Group, with generous assistance from the Friends of Beamish and other well-wishers. This process occupied over twenty years, during which time the trolleybus would appear from time to time running on the short demonstration wiring, to the delight of those who remembered using it. From 2005 until 2012, 501 operated on short-term loan to the Sandtoft Transport Centre, near Doncaster, where it operated on a number of summer season public open days, including North-East Weekends and Six-wheeler Weekends. Sub-loans were also arranged to the Black Country Museum and the East Anglia Transport Museum, thus 501 is now the only trolleybus to have operated on all four UK preserved trolleybus systems.

# Other vehicles

In addition to the fleet already described, there are a number of other artefacts which form part of the longer term plans for the Museum's tramway.

# Newcastle & Gosforth 49

Newcastle & Gosforth 49 was built by the Midland Railway Carriage & Wagon Company, probably in 1875. The N&G tramway opened in 1878 and grew into a system totalling some 12 route miles. The double deck open top 49 was sold upon closure, complete with running gear and with another horse car, for use as a summer house near Belford in Northumberland. In 1972 it was recovered to Beamish and stored. Sadly, outdoor storage and the age and fragility of 49 resulted in the tram deteriorating dramatically until it was passed to an enthusiast on Merseyside who dismantled and recorded the remains. These were returned to Beamish in April 2012.

*Photograph: Peter Barlow*

# Gateshead 51

Gateshead 51 very much fulfils the description 'long-term project'! The remaining saloon was recovered from the Ravensworth Estate on Lobley Hill in 2006, in the process being dismantled into components that were either potentially reusable or which could act as a pattern. 51 was rebuilt by Gateshead Tramways in 1920, utilising 45, itself built by the Electric Railway and Tramway Carriage Works in Preston in 1901 and not to be confused with 25, which was rebuilt and took the number 45! Renumbered 51 in 1925, the tram was one of a pair used on the Teams route (we shall meet the other shortly). Only the original section of the saloon was salvaged and sold for further use as a greenhouse-cum-potting shed, and any reconstruction of these remains will be a very long term project.

*Photograph: Paul Jarman*

# Gateshead 52

Gateshead 52 was, like 51, a rebuild of an earlier tramcar. 7 was supplied by the Electric Railway and Tramway Carriage Works in 1901, fitted with a Brill 21E 6 ft. truck and in 'Combination' format, that is to say it had both an enclosed saloon and open benches behind the driver (much like Manchester 765, seen earlier in these pages). 7 was an early conversion to the P. A. Y. E. system – the Pay As You Enter system being fitted in 1912 - and primarily used on the Bensham and Saltwell Park route. On the 5 February 1916, 7 was ascending the formidable Bensham Bank when it paused in a passing loop to await the down-hill car to pass. The driver was informed that a fight had broken out on that tram and applied his handbrake and left 7 to walk up to assist his colleagues. More passengers were boarding 7 at the time and as a result, the now heavier tram overcame the effect of its handbrake and ran backwards down the bank, overturning at the curve into Saltwell Road and killing four pedestrians and injuring ten passengers. As a result 7 was written off, but it was to reappear in 1920, completely rebuilt (probably with a completely new body) with an enclosed saloon and open vestibules. In 1928 it was renumbered, 52, and later had windscreens added as well as an 8 ft. wheelbase Brill truck. In 1951 it was withdrawn, being purchased by driver William Southern who moved the tram to his garden at Windy Nook, Gateshead (where it was joined by a number of other ex Gateshead tramcar lower deck saloons). It is said that Mr Southern removed numerous fittings whilst 52 was still in service, later refitting them once it became his property! In 1960 the tram was presented to the Tramway Museum Society (TMS) and moved to the embryonic museum site at Crich in May 1960. For much of its preservation life 52 was stored at Clay Cross, the TMS' overflow base. In 2012, by special resolution, the TMS agreed to transfer ownership of 52 to Beamish, and it was anticipated that the remains would be returned to the north east in 2013. Restoration is earmarked to commence once the heavy overhaul of Sheffield 264 is completed.

# Blackpool Tower Wagon 749

Tower Wagon 749 was built in 1907 by the Blackpool & Fleetwood Tramroad utilising a Milnes plate frame bogie from an ex-trailer in the number series 11 – 13. Usually based at Copse Road Depot, it was the partner vehicle to Blackpool 31 (then in engineering guise as 4, later 754), taking the number 749 in January 1973. It consists of a wooden, vertically telescopic tower (to enable live-line working by the overhead engineering staff) and collapsible safety panels with a wooden ladder at one end. During conservation work carried out in 2010 original B&F lettering was found beneath the later Blackpool Corporation lettering, making 749 a very precious artefact. Purely a cosmetic item, it is presently stored in the Regional Museum Store where the environmental

conditions are such that they ensure 749 remains in excellent condition pending the day it can be placed on public display.

## Leamington & Warwick 8

In August 2012 Leamington & Warwick 8 arrived at Beamish, the plan being to incorporate it with 49 to make one complete horse tram. 8 was one of a pair that had survived in Warwickshire later being recovered to the Birmingham Railway Museum at Tyseley. Later, 8 was moved to Summerlee where it was thought it might have connections with the Glasgow Corporation horse tramway, though this was later discounted. Some restoration work has been undertaken on 8, though this has removed the chance to understand much of the L&W history. Coincidentally, it is of identical design to 49.

*Photograph: Paul Jarman*

# Chapter 7:
## The operation of Beamish Tramway, and the next forty years

Operation of a heritage tramway on the scale of the Beamish Tramway is challenging for the staff and the volunteers. A small, permanent staff supports the routine maintenance and inspection work of the tramcars and tramway. The staff can call upon the expertise and knowledge of the Beamish Tramway Group, again a small but highly active team which carries out specialist works to support the Museum-led projects as well as carrying out substantial projects in its own right. Thus the tramway has been able to develop to its present size and scale of operation.

*Sunderland 16 and Newcastle 114 in the Town Street. Both were rebuilt from very few remains and both have enabled Beamish to operate local tramcars of types otherwise lost to preservation. The remains of Gateshead 51 and 52 will represent a similar challenge to the restorers but scenes like this are a reminder of the rewards for such work.* **Jason Cross**

Generally there is a minimum of two trams in service on any given day, increasing to four for peak times. Each is manned by a driver and conductor who are drawn from a pool of staff and volunteers who are trained for both tramcar and bus crewing duties and are medically examined according to DVLA standards and externally examined by (at the time of writing) an examiner from Blackpool Transport Services. All crews are supplied with a uniform (a large stock of which was derived from former Police officer costume) and each tram is subject to daily checks before entering service. A daily log is also kept and this is used by the maintenance staff to identify faults or failures as part of their routine examinations. Staff and volunteers are indistinguishable in service and both are equally proud and enthusiastic about their role and responsibility when navigating the tramway.

The Beamish Tramway Group (BTG) is formed around a small nucleus of local electric traction experts, devotees and enthusiasts drawn from a variety of engineering disciplines. As well as a focus on the tramcars and electrical infrastructure, most also fulfil an operational role driving and conducting on the tramway.

The overall operational management, curatorial guidance and liaison with the BTG falls to Paul Jarman, the Head of Transport & Industry, who also ensures that the respective statutory requirements of the tramway are met, largely though the Safety Management System, Maintenance System and Rule Book. This role also coordinates future development between all interested parties, and it is perhaps fitting to close this review of forty years of development with a look ahead to some of the future plans at the Museum that will have a bearing on the tramway.

An ambitious future plan is being developed for Beamish. This includes expansion of the existing tram/bus depot, construction of a 1950s period bus depot (possibly with accommodation for tramcars and trolleybuses) to the south east of the existing Town area, construction of a trolleybus route around the perimeter road and through a proposed 1950s urban area (approximately 1.5 miles in total route mileage), enhancement of the current engineering facilities and the restoration of additional vehicles for use on both the tramway and the trolleybus route. Initially, efforts will focus on the heavy overhaul of Sheffield 264, with Gateshead 52's extensive reconstruction to follow. The current running fleet will require increasingly extensive attention in the works as they grow older and if current traffic levels remain stable or even increase, and these needs will also be dovetailed into the plan. It is hoped that Sheffield 513 will return in due course, to be overhauled and perhaps work a dedicated 1950s route from the Entrance to the new development area. N&G horse tram 49 is also something that would enhance the tramway and an additional crossover east of the Town Street would enable short horse tram workings to operate through the street as well as 1950s turn-backs from the Entrance – thus protecting the Edwardian ambiance of the Town Street and sparing the trams with longer fixed wheelbase the punishment of wear caused by the reverse curves in this area.

Such plans are, without funding, just pipedreams. But if the last forty years is anything to judge by, the future of the Beamish Tramway is certainly one which will be just as exciting, ground-breaking and essential to the overall function of the Museum as a whole. Without a doubt future editions of this booklet will have much change to record!

*Gateshead 52 hard at work in its home town. Though some years from once again appearing in this condition, such views can inspire the work required to convert a derelict hulk into a pristine working tramcar once again.*
**George Hearse**

# Chapter 8:
# Maintaining the Fleet

We have seen the fleet in both its working and heritage guises and also seen how hard the trams at Beamish work. It is therefore imperative that the fleet is maintained in order to ensure both its longevity in service but also safety for operation. There are also curatorial considerations and sometimes research after the initial restoration reveals details that can be changed or corrected on the tramcars. Newcastle 114's livery was a case in point here, whilst 31 also received a revised livery when it was repainted in 2010. It is generally hoped that a tramcar will last as many as 20 years between heavy overhaul, sometimes more. Interim overhauls are now carried out to help towards this ambition, such work including a body lift, re-profiling of tyres, motor overhauls and general attention to those areas not normally treated within a cycle of maintenance undertaken on each tram each time it completes six days in operation. This way each tram has a mid-life overhaul to extend its inter-heavy overhaul period to as many as 30 years.

*Newcastle 114's truck stripped for overhaul. This work was undertaken at approximately 15 years in service (in 2011) and consisted of a comprehensive inspection and attention to motors, brakes, wheelsets (and tyre profile), electrical system and bodywork. It was then fully repainted in a new version of the 1901 Newcastle Corporation Transport Livery, with new research providing the details for a revision of the livery previously carried (as seen on page 2).* **Paul Jarman**

*Newcastle 114's truck, fully reassembled and awaiting transfer to Road 1 of the depot, where lifting jacks enable the body to be elevated to a sufficient height to enable the truck to be rolled under before the body is reattached.* **Paul Jarman**

During 2012 Oporto 196 entered the workshops for a mid-life overhaul. The tyre profiles were known to be particularly worn and so the body was removed from the truck, which was in turn stripped and the wheelsets and motors sent to contractors for overhaul. Meanwhile, the body (of particularly robust design) received attention to rot, as well as repairs to the work carried out in the 1990s. The roof was re-waterproofed and new advertising boards made to reflect north east practice for advertising on single deck trams. It was decided that 196 would carry the later South Shields livery of blue and primrose, something not seen on a tram since the 1940s. In September 2012 the completed tram was rolled out of the works and entered service following a period of testing and running-in. **Paul Jarman**

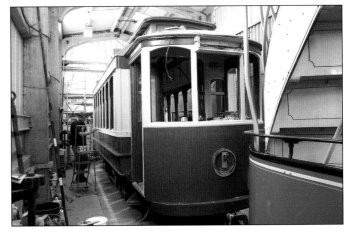

This view shows 196's transformation into South Shields livery, with undercoats presenting a much flatter appearance. The location is Road 1 of the depot, used as a workshop and painting area. **Paul Jarman**

In recent years Beamish has called upon the skills of coachpainter and signwriter Phil Anderson, who has undertaken several tramcar (and bus) repaints. He is seen here applying the black outline to the silver-leaf lining on Newcastle 114. Attention to detail with each repaint is enormously important, the appearance of the tram being what makes an immediate impression on the Museum's visitors. 114 and 196 carry particularly vibrant schemes in this regard. **Paul Jarman**

# SITE MAP

Home Farm

poultiggery

bull field

tram depot

netty

cart shed cafe

Regional Resource Centre

foulbridge

boggy close

high pasture

Pit Village

valentines close

school

chapel field

fish & chip shop

pitman's pantry

drift mine

engine shed

Colliery

Entrance Building

winding engine

birch wood

tiny tim

Pockerley Waggonway

gibbet

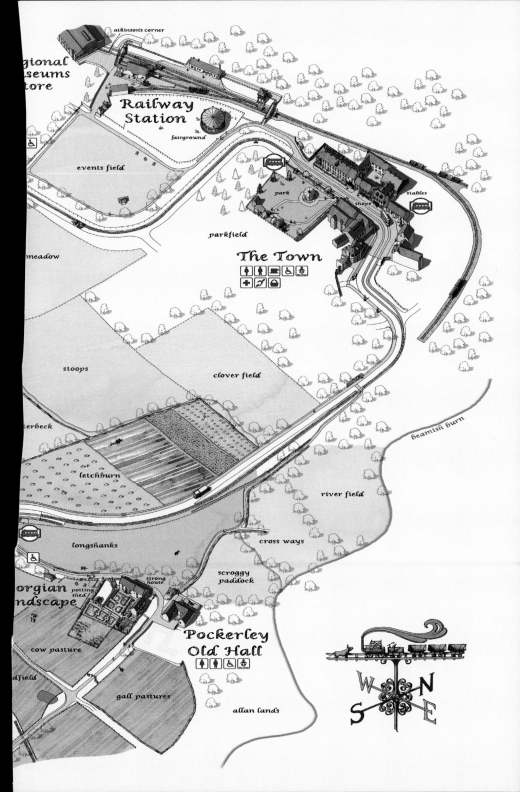

# BEAMISH MUSEUM FLEET LIST

| Fleet No. | Former Operators | Year Built | Truck/Chassis Fitted |
|---|---|---|---|
| **Horse Trams** | | | |
| 8 | Newcastle & Gosforth Tramway | 1880 | 4w |
| 49 | Leamington & Warwick Tramway | 1880 | 4w |
| **Electric Trams** | | | |
| 16 | Sunderland Corporation Tramways | 1900/1922 | Peckham P35 4w |
| 114 | Newcastle Corporation Tramways | 1901 | Brill 21E 4w |
| 31 | Blackpool Corporation Tramways | 1901/1920 | 2 x Dick Kerr Preston Maguire Equal whe |
| 51 | Gateshead & District Tramways | 1901/1917 | N/A |
| 52 | Gateshead & District Tramways | 1901/1920 | Brill 21E 4w |
| 264 | Sheffield Corporation Tramways | 1907 | Peckham P22 4w |
| 10 | Gateshead & District Tramways | 1925 | 2 x Brill 39E (Reversed) |
| 233 | Blackpool Corporation Tramways | 1934 | 2x English Electric Equal wheel |
| 101 | Blackpool Corporation Tramways | 1934 | 2x English Electric Equal wheel |
| 196 | STCP (see notes) | 1935 | Brill 21E 4w |
| 513 | Sheffield Corporation Tramways | 1952 | Maley & Taunton hornless 588 4w |
| **Trolleybuses** | | | |
| 12 | Keighley Corporation Tramways | 1924 | Straker – Clough |
| 501 | Newcastle Corporation Transport | 1949 | Sunbeam S7 |

## Notes

1  Very little remains of original tram, however, components that survive to be incorporated into a reconstructed tram– see (2)
2  Proposed that components to be incorporated with those of L&W 8 to create one tram, numbered N&G 49
3  Restored to 1922 condition.  Originally built as 8w open top car
4  Restored to 1920 condition.  Originally built as 4w open top car with enclosed vestibules
5  Built as No.45, an open top car, in 1901. Rebuilt in 1920 and renumbered to 51 in 1925. Requires total reconstruction
6  Built as No.7 in 1901, rebuilt in 1920 and renumbered to 52 in 1928.  Transferred from TMS in 2013. Requires restoration
7  Carrying original British Railways livery from 09/2012.  Due repaint in 2013
8  On loan from Lancastrian Transport Trust. BTS No.605
9  On loan from Lancastrian Transport Trust.  Carries fictitious Sunderland livery and the No.101.  Seating reduced to 88
10  Carries South Shields livery from 09/2012
11  On loan to the East Anglia Transport Museum, Lowestoft
12  Details shown are as-withdrawn.  Much equipment is missing and remains a long-term restoration prospect